First Published November 2000

Published by Lathams of Potter Heigham
1 Cherry Lane, Anglia Square, Norwich NR3 1WA

Copyright Lathams of Potter Heigham 2000

Reference ISBN 0 9539103 0 X

# Broad Smiles

## A collection of Norfolk Yarns

## Foreword

There are many ways of spreading the true Norfolk gospel, and I have been fortunate to take advantage of several of them over the past 40 years or so.

As a broadcaster and writer closely identified with the county and its unique sense of humour, I continue to seek out new pulpits from which to preach an old but priceless message - good laughs are made to be shared.

This selection of yarns, some with whiskers on, others just beginning to sprout stubble and a few still smooth with youthfulness, have all been heard on Radio Broadland, Norwich's commercial station, in connection with adverts for Lathams of Potter Heigham. I was invited to script and present Norfolk stories to go with latest offers from the discount superstore, and it seems reasonable to suggest this partnership has been mutually beneficial.

Perhaps the best indication of its success came with an outstanding response from listeners invited to send in their favourite local yarns. I sifted through hundreds for my pick of the crop, worthy of an airing on Radio Broadland as well as generous vouchers from Lathams presented at a happy gala night at the store. Several of those 'party pieces' feature in this venture.

Of course, Norfolk stories, especially those liberally laced with dialect, were designed to be told rather than be read. Many have survived simply because they were handed down verbally from one generation to the next, often embellished for good luck on the way. That hasn't stopped champions of the Norfolk cause, myself included, attempting to commit the delicate nuances of our wit and vernacular to print, despite there being no clear rules (and insufficient vowels) for doing so.

Lathams, in their wisdom and generosity, decided to endorse a 'squit bonanza' on behalf of chuckle-chasing punters with backing for both a book and a recording. So enthusiasts can read or listen - or listen and read at the same time. Pages of Companionable Dialect. A CD of Cultural Delights. A Cracking Double in the name of our celebrated Norfolk humour.

The fact that Lathams' Managing Director, Ken Turner is so proud of his Norfolk roots must figure prominently in my vote of thanks to all concerned for bringing this cheerful enterprise to fruition.

There is a small potted history of Potter Heigham and Lathams on page 62 as well as a profile of Potter Heigham's most famous son - the incomparable Sidney Grapes, which follows on page 63.

So may there be laughter in store - and anywhere else where wholesome squit is appreciated - as these yarns play their part in keeping a proud tradition flourishing.

*Keith Skipper*

# Broad Smiles
A Collection of Norfolk Yarns

## Contents
## NORFOLK YARNS

| | |
|---|---|
| Poll Position | 6 |
| On Her Toes | 7 |
| Dog-Gone It! | 8 |
| Helpful Number | 9 |
| No Pot Luck | 10 |
| Silent Role | 11 |
| In and Out | 12 |
| Quick Change | 13 |
| Perfect Line | 14 |
| Half The Battle | 15 |
| Go By Train | 16 |
| Drop of Logic | 17 |
| Be Prepared | 18 |
| Pet Subject | 19 |
| Cover Plan | 20 |
| Close Secret | 21 |
| It Was Him! | 22 |
| Different Tune | 23 |
| Sight Test | 24 |
| Just Too Late | 25 |
| Change of Mind | 26 |
| Clean Sweep | 27 |
| Worker of Note | 28 |
| By The Horns | 29 |
| Surprise Tonic | 30 |
| Dad's Dilemma | 31 |
| Two of a Kind | 32 |
| Class Reply | 33 |
| Rest In Peace | 34 |
| Wind Direction | 35 |
| Eggsaggeration! | 36 |
| Back To Work | 37 |
| Defiant End | 38 |

| | |
|---|---|
| Too Familiar! | 39 |
| Plot Thickens | 40 |
| On The Way | 41 |
| Break It In | 42 |
| Burnt Offering | 43 |
| Off The Peg | 44 |
| Seaside Tonic | 45 |
| Fowl Play | 46 |
| High Tide | 47 |
| Quick Journey | 48 |
| Corny Offer | 49 |
| Still Life | 50 |
| Basin Blues | 51 |
| Slow Learner | 52 |
| Pay As You Churn | 53 |
| Joint Operation | 54 |
| Leave It All | 55 |
| One More? | 56 |
| Basket Case | 57 |
| Frosty Answer | 58 |
| Material Witness | 59 |
| Bargain Price | 60 |
| Precisely! | 61 |
| | |
| Potter Heigham & The Lathams Story | 62 |
| Sidney Grapes - 'The Boy John' | 63 |

# Poll Position

One of the election candidates couldn't help noticing that Horry had attended all the meetings held in the village.

On the eve of the poll he made a point of going across to have a word and to thank him for his support.

Horry cleared his throat. 'Well, bor, I hev bin tew every meetin' for all four canderdates, an' I hev studied all yar leaflets an' pearpers.'

'Jolly good show!' enthused the candidate.

'An' orl I kin say, ole partner, is thass a bloomin' good job yew carnt ALL git elected!'

# On Her Toes

Horry splashed out and took his missus to the pictures in Norwich. A big treat. During the interval he went to get the ice-creams and trod rather heavily on the toes of a posh lady further along the row.

She scowled and muttered.
On his return Horry was about to pass the same lady when he asked:
''Scuse me, ole bewty, but dint I jam on yar toes minnit or tew back?'

Expecting an apology the lady said with some indignation:
'Yes, you most certainly did.'

'Oh good' said Horry, 'Then I hev got the right row arter all!'

# Dog-Gone it!

The parson was away on holiday and so the vicar from a neighbouring parish came to take the Sunday morning service.

After his sermon he apologised for it being on the short side.

'I did have a longer one all written out, but I'm afraid my dog got into the study and chewed up several of the pages.'

As he was leaving the old verger thanked him warmly for the service and then whispered:
'I say, if ever that there dawg o' yours hev enny pups, praps yew'll give one to our parson....'

# Helpful Number

Horry had just finished his tea and was reading the paper when he had to get up to answer a knock at the door.

A stranger stood there.
'Excuse me, but does a Bertie Parker live here?'

'No, he dunt.'

'Well, would you happen to know if he happens to live on this road?'

'Yis, he dew live on this road.'

'Well then, would you happen to know at what number?'

'No - but that'll be on the door.'

# No Pot Luck

Horry got a job painting the yellow lines
on the road.

On the first day he covered 100 yards.
On the second day he managed 50 yards.
On the third day he was down to 10 yards.

'What on earth is the matter?
Why are you doing less every day?
There had better be a reasonable explanation'
said the foreman, rather angrily.

Horry looked him straight in the eye.
'Well, thass like this here. The bloomin' paint
pot's gittin' further away!'

# Silent Role

It was time for the annual village school play and Ernie had been given a part.

He was very excited and ran all the way home to tell his parents.

'Yew will cum an' see it, wunt yer?'

''Cors we will.' said Mum.

'What part hev yew got?' asked Dad.

'Oh, I play a man woss celebratin' his silver weddin' anniversary.'

'Never yew mind, boy' said Dad. 'Praps they'll gi' yew a speakin' part next year!'

# In and Out

Horry was working hard in his front garden when his old mate Fred came wandering past.
'I're just bin ter hev a look at that Spring Show down the village hall.'

'Oh ah' said Horry, 'an' what dew they charge ter go in there these days?'

'Well, I dunt rightly know cors I dint pay, yer see' Fred told him.

'How'd yew manage that, ole partner?' Horry wanted to know.

Fred soon told him:
'I walked in backards - an' they thowt I wuz a'cummin out!'

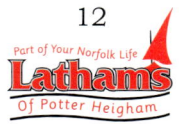

# Quick Change

There are certain advantages in travelling around Norfolk by bus.

For a start you are likely to hear some very funny things. Like this one that happened only the other day.

A very posh lady clambered up the steps, undid her purse and handed over a £10 note to the driver with a most apologetic look.

'Oh dear. I do not seem to have a 50p piece for the fare.'

The bus driver took the note.
'Dunt yew fret, my ole bewty.
In jist a minnit yew'll hev 19 of 'em!'

# Perfect Line

A couple of American servicemen were waiting for a train.

They kept on telling the old Norfolk porter how they had bigger and faster trains back home.

He just got on with his work and didn't reply.

They were just about to elaborate when a fast train to Yarmouth raced through, hauled by a Britannia class locomotive.

'Gee, buddy, what on earth was that?' asked one of the Americans.

'Oh' said the old porter in a very matter of fact way:
'I reckon that wuz ole Tom dewin' a bit o' shuntin'!'

# Half The Battle

Old Jimmy saved up to buy a bike.

He told his pals on the farm:
'Blarst, now I kin hoss over ter Swaffham
ter see my sister on Sundays.'

On the Monday morning they naturally
asked how he had got on.

'Well, by the time I git ter Dereham I wuz
proper wore out, so I tanned rownd
and cum streart hoom agin.'

'But thass only harf way' they said.

'I know' said Jimmy with a smile.
'I'll hatter dew the th'uther harf next week!'

# Go By Train

Jack was strolling across a field when he saw
Stan hoeing the sugar beet.

'What time dew yew knock orff?'

'Bowt five o'clock.'

'Hev yew got a watch?'

'No, I hent got a watch.'

'So, how dew yew know when thass time
ter knock orff?'

'Well, yew see there's a railway line over there.
A train go by at har'past five,
so if I pack up harf an hour afore that git here,
I know I'm bowt right.'

# Drop of Logic

There had been a hosepipe ban in operation and all the gardens in the village looked very parched.

All, that is, except old John's garden.

The man from the water board was rather suspicious, and so he called round to remind John that he was not allowed to use the mains water for his garden.

'Dunt yew worry yarself abowt that, my ole bewty' John told him.

'We see it like this here. When we're got plenty we use it sparingly - so when we hent got enny, we're allus got sum!'

The water board official said he thought he agreed.

# Be Prepared

Fred and Ernie were working on fields
well away from the farm.

One morning Fred turned up late.
That afternoon about half an hour before
leaving-off time, he started packing
up his things.

'Hold yew hard, ole partner!' said Ernie.
'That ent knockin'-orf tyme yit.'

'I know' said Fred, 'but I was allus told that
dunt dew ter be learte twice in one day!'

# Pet Subject

Ezra's wife was at home alone when
the insurance man called in the hope
of landing a new customer.

'Oh, I leave them sort o' things
ter my ole man' she said.

'So you don't know what you would do if your
husband died?' asked the insurance agent.

'Well, no, not zakkly' said Ezra's missus.
'But I think I'd git a budgie or a poodle.'

# Cover Plan

The farmer's maid refused to get up. The farmer, thinking she was ill, sent for the doctor.

'Now, what's the matter, Mary?'

'Ent noffin the matter.'

'Well, why don't you get up then?'

'They owe me two month's wearjes - an' I dunt git up til they pay up.'

The doctor smiled. 'Oh, is that all. Well, shift over - they've owed me a bill for over two years.'

## Close Secret

The new village parson asked old George
if he knew the best way to keep the
flock interested.

'Well, old bewty, we allus reckun
the secret of a good sarmun
is a good beginnin' an' a good endin''.

The parson smiled his thanks.
But old George hadn't quite finished....

'An' leave 'em as close tergether as possible!'

# It Was Him!

A village schoolmaster was taking
a class in history.
He asked 'Who signed Magna Carta?'

Little Bertie replied:
'If you please, sar, I dint'

Next day the teacher bumped
into Bertie's father.
'Your lad didn't half amuse us yesterday
when I asked who signed Magna Carta and he
said: 'If you please sar, I dint'.'

Bertie's dad replied with a wink
'Little beggar - I bet he did!'

# Different Tune

An old farmer was dying.
His wife and a few neighbours
were sitting by the bed.

'I owe Farmer Brown five quid'
whispered the old farmer.

His wife shrugged:
'There he go, ramblin' agin.'

After a lengthy silence, the old boy
started to whisper again:
'Farmer Harvey owe me ten quid.'

At this his wife said triumphantly:
'There he go agin - sensible to the larst!'

# Sight Test

Fred was sitting in the kitchen
taking a little rest.
His spectacles were on the table.

'You know, dear' said his wife,
'Wi'owt yar glasses on I could mistearke
yew fer the handsome young feller
I married all them years ago.'

'Funny yew should say that' Fred replied.
'Wi'owt my glasses
yew still look quite nice tew'.

# Just Too Late

'What a pretty little village!'
enthused the woman tourist to her husband.

'Let's go and ask that dear old chap
over there all about it.'

The village sage was sitting alone
outside the pub in the sunshine.

'Would you happen to be the oldest
inhabitant of this enchanting little hamlet?'
gushed the woman.

'Blarst, no' replied the old man
taking a sip of his half-pint.
'He went an' died larst week.'

# Change of Mind

Billy's bonfire got out of hand
and his garden shed was burnt down.

He went to see the insurance agent hoping
to collect the money for it.
He was told it didn't quite work like that.

'You have to fill in a claim form
and then an agent will call
and value the damage.

Anyway we don't pay out cash ...
we replace the property.'

Billy thought for a minute
'In that case, yew'd better
cancel that policy on my missus!'

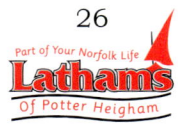

# Clean Sweep

The village roadman was having
a spot of bother as the vicar biked past.

It seemed the broom handle
had come away from the head.

On his return two hours later
the vicar was surprised to see him
still struggling. He asked what was wrong.

'Well, ole bewty, thass like this here'
said the roadman.
'I hev put the duzzy handle on twice -
an' now the hid he' cum orff.'

# Worker of Note

An agricultural worker went
to a Norfolk farm for a job.

Quite reasonably, he was asked
for a character reference
from his last employer.

'Well, marster, I did hev one but I lorst it.'

'You must be a fool, losing it like that'
said the farmer.

'Not such a fewl as yew myte think'
said the worker.
'Yew see, ole bewty, I'd read it!'

# By The Horns

The village parson was very surprised
to bump into one of his Sunday School
pupils down a narrow lane.

She was driving a large cow.

'Good morning, Mary,
where are you going with that enormous beast?'

'Please, sar, I'm a'tearkin' ole Buttercup
ter be bulled.'

'Dear me - but couldn't your father do that?'

'Oh no, sar..... that must be a bull.'

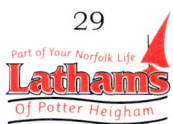

# Surprise Tonic

A rather deaf old lady,
whose sight was not too good,
complained of feeling unwell
so her granddaughter called the doctor.

As he left, the granddaughter, raising her voice,
said 'Well, Grandma, how are you feeling now?'

'A little better. It was nice of the Wikker ter call.'

'But Grandma, that was the doctor,
not the vicar.......'

'Well, blarst me!' said the old lady.
'I wuz just a'thinkin' he wuz a bit familiar!'

# Dad's Dilemma

A farmer came out of the yard to find
a worried looking lad standing beside
an overturned load of hay.
'Dunt yew worry, boy.
I'll get a couple o'my chaps ter pitch it back.'

'But what'll father say?'

'Dew yew cum in an hev a glass of beer
while they're loading up.'

'But what'll father say?'

'Blarst, boy, what are yew a' worryin'
abowt yer father for?'

'Cors he's under the hay!'

# Two of a Kind

An old carpenter working at
the local doctor's house was putting putty
in his joints to make a good fit.

The doctor said:
'I suppose a piece or two of putty
has covered up several of your mistakes, George.'

'Yis, Doctor' replied the carpenter.
'An' I bet a sod or two o' grass
hev covered up savrul o' yors anorl!'

# Class Reply

A special inspector went to a Norfolk village school many years ago to investigate reports of low standards.

He questioned a boy he considered none too bright.

'Now, I walked down a road 200 yards wide and half a mile high. How old am I?'

The boy replied immediately '42, Sir.'

This was absolutely correct.
But how did he arrive at the answer?

'Well, thass like this here..... I got a brother at home woss 21 - and he's only harf a fule!'.

# Rest In Peace

An old Norfolk countryman went into
a chemist's shop on market day
and ordered a large bottle of sleeping pills.

'Gimme the biggest yew're got - dunno what I'd
dew wi'out them' he confided.
'I'd never get a night's rest, thass fer sure.'

The girl behind the counter warned him not to
take too many at once.

The old boy replied:
'Cor blarst, I dunt tearke 'em myself -
I give them ter my ole gal.'

# Wind Direction

A motorist taking a short cut through country lanes in Norfolk came to a main road where he found a signpost to Norwich. But it was pointing in the opposite direction to what he had expected.

An old man, clearly a local, wandered towards him and said:
'Dunt yew tearke enny notice o' that ole pust - thass loose.

When the wind's in the east,
Norwich lay over there.
When thass in the west,
Norwich lay over here........'

# Eggsaggeration!

They were mardling in the local.
Bill told Horry his hens lay two eggs a day each.

'Well' said Horry, 'When I wuz in the Navy,
we wuz in the Med an' we hed a day orff.
Sum on us went swimmin' an' we dived
an' found an old Spanish galleon.
On the stern were tew gret ole lanterns
wi' the candles still alight.'

'Dunt tork such squit!' said Bill.

'Right yew are' said Horry.

'Yew harf yar egg producshun
an' I'll blow my candles out!'

# Back To Work

A Norfolk farmer was waiting
for his men to arrive for work
on a very frosty morning.

One chap had to walk two miles across the fields.
The farmer asked him why he was late.

'That bloomin' footpath wuz so slippery
every time I took a step forrard
I skidded back two.'

'Well,' said the farmer,
'How did you get here then?'

The chap replied:
'Blarst, I tanned rownd an' went hoom!'

# Defiant End

An elderly Norfolk couple had led
a cat and dog existence and hadn't spoken
to each other for years.

The husband fell ill and lay dying.
His wife, anxious for a reconciliation
before it was too late, decided
to make the first move.

She went upstairs to the old man's bedside and,
breaking the long silence
between them, whispered:

'George, where dew yew want ter be buried?'

The answer came back without hesitation
and in a voice full of malice:

'On top o' yew!'

# Too Familiar!

A group of hikers approached an old Norfolk
labourer as he leaned over a gate,
and the leader asked if they were
on the right road to Yarmouth.

Seconds later, shocked at the language and the
way in which the old man threatened
to set his dog on them, they beat a hasty retreat.

'Tryin' ter mearke a fule outter me!'
muttered the old man.
'Askin' the way ter Yarmouth loike that.
Dint think I recognised 'em.

Blarst, that chap asked me the
searme thing only tew year ago!'

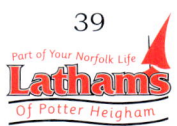

# Plot Thickens

Billy was in prison for something he didn't do -
he didn't wear gloves.

He knew all mail in and out of the
prison was censored.
He got a letter from his wife asking
'When do I plant the spuds?'

He wrote back: 'Dunt yew dig up our garden.
Thass where I buried all that money!'

His wife wrote back a few days later
'Six policemen come an' dug up every
square inch of the back garden.'

By return of post she got the answer:
'Rite, now yew kin plant the spuds!'

# On The Way

A young girl from Potter Heigham
sought her grandfather's approval for a rather
short outfit she had bought to wear
over the festive season.

'What dew yew think o' my rig-out, then?
Dew yew think thass becummin?'

The old man drew on his pipe and looked
at her for a few moments.

'Well, my gal,' he replied,
'that might be cummin -
but when will that git here?'

# Break It In

A farmworker from Potter Heigham called at a harness makers in the village regarding a horse collar he had ordered as a present.

'Yew know that ole collar yew med for our ole mare? That ent big enuff. I carnt git it onto har cors that 'oont go over har lugs.'

The harness maker replied: 'Well, yew'll be able ter git it onto har arter she're wore it a few times.'

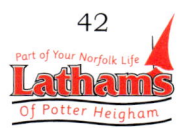

# Burnt Offering

Billy's missus wasn't the best
of performers in the kitchen.

Her Norfolk dumplings were invariably
sinkers rather than swimmers.

But she did try very hard when it came to
preparing a special family dinner.

Billy looked at it disdainfully as she brought it in,
noting burnt pastry around a meat pie.

'Blarst, gal, I dunt mind eatin' hoss flesh - but I
dunt want the hoss collar ter go with it!'

# Off The Peg

Billy's missus went Christmas shopping
in Potter Heigham and spent a lot
of money on his presents.

She hid them in the bottom of the wardrobe -
and asked what he was going to buy her.

'A new spin-dryer, my bewty'
he answered proudly.

On Christmas morning she opened the present
and let out a howl of despair
'Yew sorft ole tewl!'

Billy's spin-dryer was a true Norfolk model - a
hoola hoop with linen pegs!

# Seaside Tonic

Horry's brother came for a visit from the big city.
'Where would like to go for a day out?'
he asked him.

'I would like to take a stroll round Potter Heigham
and then head for the coast'
said the brother.

After a minute the visitor asked
'Is the Norfolk coast still good for arthritis?'

'Oh yis' said Horry.
'I only went there twice … and I got it!'

# Fowl Play

Charlie called at the village shop
to buy a dozen eggs.

As the shopkeeper went to serve him,
Charlie exclaimed:
'Hold yew hard! I want the ones what the
yeller-legged hens lay.'

With a puzzled look the shopkeeper
told Charlie that if he had any way
of telling which ones they were,
he could pick them out himself.

He did.

He picked out the biggest dozen he could find.

# High Tide

George and Billy went for a day out
at the seaside.
They ate their sandwiches on the beach.

Billy finished drinking his cold tea and
then wandered down to the sea to
fill his bottle with water.

'What are yew a'dewin'?' said George.

'Well, my missus hent sin the sea fer years,
and I thowt I'd tearke sum onnit hoom fer har.'

'Yew silly owl fewl' said George.
'When the tide cum in that'll bust the bottle!'

# Quick Journey

It was the day of the funeral
of a Norfolk woman who had been
thoroughly disliked in the village.

She had henpecked her husband,
driven her children mercilessly
and picked arguments with all the neighbours.

As the service ended a violent storm broke.
There was a blinding flash of lightening followed
by a terrific clap of thunder.

'Cor, blarst me' said old Jack,
stroking his chin thoughtfully,
'Dint tearke har long ter git there!'

# Corny Offer

A young mechanic was called out to a Norfolk farm at harvest time to mend the binder.

It was a very tricky job to be carried out in sweltering conditions.

The farmer eventually turned to the mechanic and inquired: 'Dew yew drink?'

'Yis, that I dew' came the expectant reply.

'Good' said the farmer drily, 'that should help keep the price of barley up.'

# Still Life

George and Billy were having a mardle
while leaning on the church wall
overlooking the graveyard.

'Billy, where would yew like ter lay
when the time cum?'

'In that corner, next to old Passy Smith.
He wuz a good sort. What bowt yew?
Where would yew like ter lay?'

"Long sider Florrie Walker
under that ole oak tree.'

'Hold yar row - she ent dead yit!'

'I know that - an nor arn't I!'

# Basin Blues

The vicar went to the old lady's house
and found her boiling pea soup and bone broth
on the hob. He caught a whiff and said:

'Ummmmmm! How I would like
a drop of that, my dear'

He sat relishing the culinary delights
when a little pig came in,
squealing and rubbing against his legs.

After a time the vicar remarked:
'What a friendly little chap.'

The old girl smiled
'Yis, an he know yew're got his basin!'

# Slow Learner

Tom won most of the prizes as usual
at the local horticultural show.

The vicar presented him with his cups
and asked him how he did it.

'Manewer' said Tom.
'Good, rotten manewer.'

Tom went off. The vicar turned to Tom's wife.
'He is truly a marvellous gardener, but I wish you
could teach him to call it fertiliser
rather than manure.'

'I'll dew my best, wikker,' said Mabel
'but that took me thatty year ter git
him ter say manewer.'

# Pay As You Churn

A Norfolk farmer and his wife went
into the bank with a milk churn
and heaved it up to the counter.

'We'd like ter start a bank account, ole partner'
said the farmer, lifting the lid to show
the churn full of coins.

It took the cashier over three hours to count it.

When she told the farmer how much,
he exclaimed: 'That can't be right.
That's thateen quid short.'

His wife went red ......
'Yew know what we're dun, dunt yer -
we're gorn an' bort the wrong churn.'

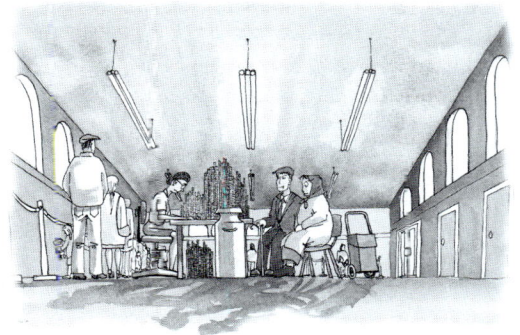

# Joint Operation

Old Harry was busy tending his garden
when the new parson looked over the hedge
and called out enthusiastically:

'My word, what a splendid job you
and the Lord have made of that blessed plot.
It's a real delight to see it.'

Harry laid down his spade, wiped his hands and
walked slowly over to
where the parson was standing.

'Well, my ole bewty, yew orter hev sin this lot
when the Lord hed it on his own!'

# Leave It All

Two Norfolk mawthers decided to have a day
shopping in Norwich.

They were all excited as they caught the morning
train. Then they settled back to
plan the day ahead.

Suddenly, one turned to the other and said:
'Ethel, you know when yar
grandfather died……..?'

'Yeh ….'

'Well, how much munny did he leave?'

'Oh' said Ethel after a long pause,
'All of it - yew hev to.'

# One More?

The parson went with members of his
Church Women's Group on their outing to
Burnham Thorpe, Lord Nelson's birthplace.

On the way they stopped at
a village for a short break

A local, seeing the bus load of women
and only one man, said:
'What are yew goin' ter dew with
all them wimmun?'

The vicar replied:
'We're going to Burnham, my man'.

'To burn'em, are yew? Jist yew wait a minute,
marster. I'll go an' git my ole woman!'

# Basket Case

An old Norfolk farmer was out early one
morning strolling across his land.

Suddenly a hot air balloon came
drifting across the field.

A rather posh voice from the balloon said:
'Excuse me, good sir.
Could you tell me exactly where I am?'

The farmer looked up and without
the blink of an eye replied:

'Ah, yew carn't fewl me .....
yew're in that there barskit.'

# Frosty Answer

It was a bitterly cold morning
when the foreman arrived on site to
see one of his road gang leaning on his shovel.

He went up to Billy and asked:
'Would you rather be frozen to death
or worked to death?'

Billy thought for a moment
and then replied without the hint of a smile:

'Dunt yew worry, marster.
I kin stand the cold fairly well.'

# Material Witness

Old Joe stood in the dock accused
of poaching pheasants.

He'd been sleeping rough and so
his clothes were none too clean.

The judge looked at Joe over his spectacles
and remarked: 'Goodness, gracious, my good
man, how long do you wear your shirts?'

Joe's reply was instant:
'Six inches below m' backside, yer honour.
How long dew yew wear yars?'

# Bargain Price

It had been a bad year for potatoes
but Horry grew his own and had a good crop.
He decided to sell them from a little table at his
front gate for 60p a pound.

A lady, a renowned bargain-hunter,
looked at the price and said:
'The fellow on the market is selling
his at 50p a pound.'

'Well,' said Horry,
'why dint yew get them orff him?'

'He'd sold out' said the woman.

Back came Horry, quick as a flash:
'Well, when I're sold out I sell 'em
for 50p a pound as well.'

# Precisely!

A posh old boy in his big car on the way to
Latham's of Potter Heigham
pulled up beside a man laying
paving slabs on the pavement.

He wound his window down and said:
'We have similar jobs, you know.
I am a brain surgeon and I have to work
within one thousandth of an inch.'

'Well,' said the chap laying the slabs,
'Yew wunt be enny good on this job then ....
I hev ter be spot-on!'

# Potter Heigham & The Lathams Story

As far back as 1900, Potter Heigham was famous as the Norfolk Broads holiday destination linked by railway to the Midlands. Visitors would return year on year to take the Norfolk air and to meet up with the locals they had come to know on first name terms. Many returned during August each year when the annual Potter Heigham Regatta was held - hundreds of boats, fairs and thousands of visitors made it one of the events on the Broads during the year.

Boat building has been established for many decades at Potter Heigham with the famous Applegate Boatyard and the Herbert Woods Boatyard, established in the early 1900's and still present opposite Lathams to this day. This boatyard started building and operating the first Broads cruisers at the turn of the century. During the war they were commissioned to build motor torpedo boats and at one time also built lifeboats to be used aboard HMS Shackelton. Another famous customer of the boatyard included George Formby who lived in nearby Wroxham.

The Lathams story begins in 1963 when Ken Latham opened the general store - known as 'Aladins Cave". Lathams used to stock everything for the holidaymaker and visiting fisherman, even supplying grocery orders to cruisers who had moored up nearby.

Today Potter Heigham has lost none of it's charm. It is still one of the most popular places to visit on the Norfolk Broads - whether as a centre for cruising holidays, a perfect place to hire day boats, or simply to watch the boats go by. Even Lathams itself has grown to be a major attraction in its own right.

By sheer coincidence, Potter Heigham was also home to one of Norfolk's original rustic comedians - Sidney Grapes. You can read all about Sidney on the opposite page.

# Sidney Grapes (1888 - 1958)
# The Boy John

The most endearing of local characters, Sidney Grapes made his mark as a rustic comedian at local concerts and dinners. But he will be most fondly remembered for the Boy John letters he sent to the Eastern Daily Press from 1946 until his death in 1958.

Sidney lived all his life in the Broadland village of Potter Heigham, where he ran a garage business. The letters were composed by a countryman who wrote as he spoke and spelt as he pleased, and featured the Boy John, Granfar, Aunt Agatha and the scandalous Oul Mrs W---. Perhaps the letters were more eagerly anticipated because they were infrequent. Sidney was pressed to become a regular weekly contributor, but he was as wary of the blandishments of journalism as he was of the professional stage.

Many readers "cheated" and always went to the P.S. first for Aunt Agatha's latest example of homespun philosophy - P.S. Aunt Agatha she say, "The more you say, the less people remember." Collections of the Boy John letters have sold in their thousands over the years, and retain their freshness simply because of the way they were drawn from the heart of Norfolk village life. In his address at the dedication service at Potter Heigham Church on Sunday November 23rd 1958, the Bishop of Norwich, the Rt Rev Percy Herbert, said: "It is not given to many writers to create fictitious characters that are so alive, and that once met will never be forgotten... To read those letters is really to be enriched, and then to go on our way with the new courage and they breathe all the time, and a new joy in our hearts that we should be alive...He was not only an astonishingly fine natural humourist, he was an incomparable teller of good stories."

P.S One year, a few weeks before Christmas, Sidney Grapes put this notice on his garage window at Potter Heigham: "A Happy Christmas to all my customers whot hev paid their bills, and a prosperous New Year to them whot hent."

You can order further copies of this book or the accompanying Norfolk Yarns CD via mail order by telephoning (01603) 724804.

CREDITS
Yarns compiled by Keith Skipper.
Illustrations by Sam Robbins.
Cover photography by Sam Robbins.
Design & artwork by ETT Marcoms.

Copyright: Lathams of Potter Heigham November 2000